# Ships

Written by Charlotte Raby

Illustrated by Moreno Chiacchiera

**Collins**

# a quick ship

# a pink ship

a quick ship

a pink ship

# this ship has sunk

# a thin red fish

this ship has sunk

a thin red fish

# a big ship

# a long box

a big ship

a long box

# ✾ Review: After reading ✾

Use your assessment from hearing the children read to choose any GPCs or words that need additional practice.

## Read 1: Decoding
- Turn to pages 2 and 3. Ask the children to read the words and to point to the word that ends with the sound /nk/ (*pink*).
- Turn to pages 6 and 7. Ask the children what sound is at the end of the last word on each page. (*/nk/ **sunk** and /sh/ **fish***)
- Turn to page 11 and ask the children to find a word that ends with the sound /ng/ (*long*).

## Read 2: Vocabulary
- Go back over the book and discuss the pictures. Encourage children to talk about details that stand out for them. Use a dialogic talk model to expand on their ideas and recast them in full sentences, as naturally as possible.
- Work together to expand vocabulary by naming objects in the pictures that children do not know.
- Turn to page 4 and ask: Which word means the opposite of slow? (*quick*) Repeat for pages 10 and 11: Which word means the opposite of little? (*big*) Which word means the opposite of short? (*long*)

## Read 3: Comprehension
- On pages 2 and 3, ask: Which is the **quick ship**? Which is the **pink ship**?
- Say: Point to the ship that no one can sail in now. Why can't people sail in it? (e.g. *it has sunk*)
- Turn to pages 14 and 15 and look at the picture together.
   o Ask the children to describe what they can see and to tell you anything they can about the different types of ships.
   o Ask: Which ship would you most like to explore? Why?